BOA
EDITIONS
LIMITED

THE NIGHT PATH

Poems by
Laurie Kutchins

BOA Editions, Ltd. ☆ Rochester, NY ☆ 1997

LC #: 97–72085
ISBN: 1–880238–48–9 cloth
ISBN: 1–880238–49–7 paper

First Edition
97 98 99 00   7 6 5 4 3 2 1

Publications by BOA Editions, Ltd.—
a not-for-profit corporation under section 501 (c) (3)
of the United States Internal Revenue Code—
are made possible with the assistance of grants from
the Literature Program of the New York State Council on the Arts,
and the Literature Program of the National Endowment for the Arts,
the Lannan Foundation, the Sonia Raiziss Giop Charitable Foundation,
the Eric Mathieu King Fund of The Academy of American Poets,
as well as from the Rochester Area Foundation Community Arts Fund
administered by the Arts & Cultural Council for Greater Rochester,
the County of Monroe, NY,
and from many individual supporters.

Cover Design: Geri McCormick
Cover Art: "Nude & Landscape #8" by Miriam Garcia
Author Photo: Terry Wild
Typesetting: Richard Foerster
Printed in the United States by McNaughton and Gunn
BOA Logo: Mirko

BOA Editions, Ltd.
Alexandra Northrop, Chair
A. Poulin, Jr., President, Founder (1976–1996)
260 East Avenue
Rochester, NY 14604

for Weston

We are in love lightly, lightly. We know we are shining
Though we cannot see one another.

—James Wright, "Yes, But"

Contents

☆
☆
☆

☆
☆
☆

☆
☆
☆

THE NIGHT PATH

Prelude

All day long it has snowed and rained and snowed.
I kept a fire going in a stone hut
under the green apron of an old pine
that has seen so much more than this.
When it snowed the mud of the road whitened,
and I sensed how something near death
grows toward an ancient silence, how like a newborn
it begins to shine with the loss of markings.
The snow worked hard to cover wheel and animal tracks,
to make the road and the hills look as if no one
had ever passed here. They were getting ready for you,
like a page waiting for music.

Then the snow fell to rain, pulling the long grass down,
rubbing the white road until mud showed through
in letter shapes like brands on the hinds of cattle.
Only twice I heard a truck pass. The road changed again.
I watched two field mice lug the hard bread I tossed
from lunch into their cache under the porch.
I want you to know these small things add up
to something that won't take a name. They matter
even while the world burns human fires.

I cannot tell you why I love the snow,
why I want it to keep falling all day and night
for the next two months and fill the world
before you slip into it. I hear the rain drip from the roof,
the light snow falling, and you rounding my belly
as if you understood the moon. This is the seventh month.
Your ears, barely the size of coat buttons, hear me.
Your legs and arms have less drifting space.
Your eyes can tell the difference now between light and dark.
You dream. But I want you to know nothing.

Not even consciousness will prepare you for the light
and dark of my world. I have spoken to no one
but you all day. It is time to cross the white road,
wander into the opening eye and make the first markings.
I will wait a few more moments until it is fully dark.
The path will be a lavender sash of snowlight.
We will put our cheeks to the cheek
of whatever all this day has been listening.

Afternoon Along the Firehole River

Lying face up in the grass
that grows thick along the Firehole River, I am surrounded
by the amber births
of dragonflies.

Ravenous, like a string of sixteenth notes, they speed
up and down, feeding on things I cannot see
on the surface of the
warm current.

Thinking my nose is a sure stone, one pauses momentarily there—
I see close-up wings as sheer as a dress
I would wear made of 1920's
silk crepe.

They leave no sound in the eardrum of the afternoon.

I feel the present breeze on my forearms, then the deep snows,
the hooves and tongues of animals
who in the dead
of winter

find the river, its heat, its perfect islands of grass, stand
with forelegs pressed against the rush
and piss
and drop their necks to the green mirage

of summer. I feel the tongues of the first trappers
who trapped themselves in this water
and in one breath blessed
and cursed it.

This is death licking me all over
until I rise wobbly and
unsure of the summer air, and enter
the river,
half fire from inside the earth, half snow melt.

My head drops into the braid of it, my body flows out
beyond me, my old shape in the grass
gleaming and strewn and
weightless
among the various husks.

☆
☆
☆

Birthdream (1)

This time I had given birth
to a child with a dark, remarkable tail.
Part animal, part girl.
I wanted no one to see her,
not even the father. I wanted my privacy
to put her back inside me,
back through the glop of the birth-neck,
into the bluish glue my body had made
for her for seven months. It was not time,
she must wait, come back
when the animal had been outgrown. I held her briefly
in my arms and stroked her tail before
we parted, her eyes
nursing the dark moons.

She was never my daughter, and yet
she brought
her own wild light
into the room so that when I opened my eyes
at daybreak,
the first thing I saw was snow
spinning small
shoulders in the windows.

The last I saw of her.

☆
☆ ☆

Taurus

In the last weeks that boundary is effaced, useless
as a wind-sagged wire fence. Each hour the body grows
more dilatory, stunned into sluggish, lost sense.
I know now why the bloated heifer went off by herself
that spring morning, across the mud-hoofed snow path,
stood stiffly among the twisted cottonwoods
and watched from her distance the herd cluster and form
the feeding line behind the team-drawn flatbed
from which we broke and dropped cold bound hay;
then turned her head away, toward a sniff of water,
tail erect, the thin bag floating like a clear balloon
as she worked deeper into shadow, flared
her messy eyes when we neared, and birthed
the stubborn bull calf on her own the hour we went inside
the calving hut, out of the wind to warm up, cook breakfast.

September First

The sky turned over sometime in the night.
While it happened I slept
under a quilt of geese. My throat

felt their beaks utter
a parched *goodbye* to the dulled gold
surfaces of summer.

This morning the aspen leaves lean toward me.
They are speaking to one another with an intimacy
I've never known.

When did I first hear the elk's
seasonal love-call,
resonant out of the ghost of dusk?

Who taught me to read the sky?
Twitch of a licked index finger.
A page turned in the dark.

My Father's Tumor

It comes to me out of nowhere, always an image
of what it is not, long after dusk in summer
when I swing alone on the pine swing
and the moon is in another world.
I crane my neck back to watch stars cluster
across the sky, they could be cells within the body
of night, which makes me smaller than a cell—but what?
Or it looms across the afternoon, white anvil cumulus
storing the night storms. Sometimes it arrives uninvited,
when touching should obliterate image, when the lover
who is only a benign likeness to the father,
binds the distance.

It troubles me how I have to chase his tumor away,
how it returns with its prod of memory,
its associative powers, its disturbing attachments
to the things in this world I try to simply love.
What would it be like to live without connections,
without likenesses, and offsprings?
Twice the doctors have cut his tumor out, but it came back
in other places in the body. The third time
they boiled it away with poisons that swam hard upstream,
like salmon into the natal chambers of blood.
What is it like to live without a future?

Sometimes I think his tumor must be the past,
the way it keeps appearing and disappearing,
a gnarl of memory to be snipped away.
But each time it comes back
tenacious as a fist, I begin to wonder
if it is, after all, the future—nomadic, disassociated,
floating in fluid like a misformed embryo in a jar.
I think it is my own vagrant anger
with no place to go but home.

It has come home to make him live,
for once, with forgiveness and tenderness
while he has time. To heal him
and to kill him.

Prayer

White heart of snowlight
                              white ash in the hut grate
insects asleep in the woodbed
                              snowdrift feather of the nuthatch
woodpecker warbler woodthrush finch
                              winter's lost glove
crosshatched shadow in the meadow soft
                                        ooze of
earth out of corn snow
                    corn out of earth
                                   rounds to greenswell

an unremembered dream floats across the meadow
                                             out and back
and the fox who is like the snow
                         slips into formlessness
into shadow sense
                    rootward
                              bird
                                        ancestral spirit
                 two-syllable duet
          da-doo
                         da-doo

What is the name for the thawing morning
                    midwinter spring   or spring?
What is it about a season in labor
                    that changes the way we breathe
draws it out of us as if to help it along
          birth breath
                    death breath
                              crow and stork.

And from whom did I learn to pray to linear time?
I must unwind the prayer that was chanted in my ear.
I must unbless it,
              lay it strand by strand
                        over the first limb
                                  like ceremonial hair
a free-for-all for the nest-gathering birds.

The morning is round with their singing to one another
back and forth
              across the meadow sun
                da-doo
                          da-doo

a branch in the white birch whose skin
                        curls and floats away
a crack in the dead oak
                inhabited by orange lichen
    live moss
            a colony of spore tongues.

Or maybe it is only one bird
                singing to itself
                        traversing the meadow
so fast no one sees it, one only hears it
                filling both parts of the duet
                  you-who
      you-who
I would like to fill my mornings by singing to someone
                        who sings back to me
    who sings back
              even if it is me
                  singing inside me.

My body is rounder and heavier from love than it has ever been
my hands in love with the roundness
                even the month is lunar-round

the fused lids of the unborn have reopened
the eyes blink and fathom the light of morning on my skin
                    they twist from side to side
                                  with a readiness
the eyelashes spin and flutter
                  from a liquid strand
                        they fathom the thaw

my veins have thickened into blue determined rivers
my ankles and breasts are estuaries of blood
nipples dark as berry juice the cervix
                           a sleeping bridge
the road down my belly smells the coming mud
we are one body
          the thaw of an animal
                      the heat
making its own prayer
            a breathing in the navel hole

my intellect will have nothing to do with this birth
it is the animal
              sluggish with pregnancy and winter
                          yessing the sun

I Wanted to Paint the Night

I wanted to paint the night:
the glow that comes from nowhere
the yearly spill of lilacs
filling an open window
moonless streetlampless shine
the eyes adjust to
after the snuffed yellow smudge of lamp oil
loses its afterscent   after the bodies of lovers
slip back into separateness
and the newborn sniffs out the milky
tit alert inside the gown
and the ears adjust to the still blue
breath falling on cattle
on hills windless as closed eyelids
and there comes a memory
of counting stars from the cold bed of a truck
a memory of giving up
the long lulls between trains
the sound of a dog that chases rabbits
in its sleep and a green-eyed black cat
moving from one room to another
like a dream we usually sleep through
unless   like me
you wanted to paint
the night's own light
thin   plum   skin

Two Dreamers

1.

In the few places in this meadow
where the sun has not found its way,
the grass is still brittle and white from the night frost.
I walk in those footprints, among the long-needled pines,
half of me held by sunlight,
half by blue shadow.

My footprints will make sense to none
but the fox who started to cross the meadow
a few moments ago. I saw
her front paws flicker
toward sunlight as if for the first time,
her breath drifted like my own
into the morning.   I stopped.
                              She stopped.
We pulled the translucent strand between us,
the clear thread that makes her almost human,
me almost animal, her face
turned toward me, her muzzle
twitching and clutching my scent.
Her ears intuited my stillness,
no part of her fooled.
                        I came close as I ever have
before she veered politely, her orange tail
springing back to a shadow
under the fir trees. My footprints
will make sense to none but the night,
its traces of frost, its shoeless children.

This is how it is for me, waking,
standing at the edge of a meadow where something already
happened, my dreams seeping into my skin
before I remember
how I came here.

2.

There are two dreamers in me.
The fetus turning under my heart,
held in place by braids of blood and fluid,
already dreams on its own.
In the last phase of its darkness I lay awake,
my hands roam my belly,
my fingertips tap small notes through my skin.
It moves in me as moonlight in the elm,
leaves turning under wind.
Never has my heart worked so hard
for the two of us,
and it is dreaming, a raindrop fattened under the eaves,
its fingers and limbs and eyelids learning to swim
toward its own life.

Other nights, when I am dreaming, it wakes and flips,
blinks and sucks, kicks its small sea,
rows from one side of me to the other,
alert in the lethargic night shift
of shared blood.
Its fingers tap small rhythms through my skin,
its elbows knock, it hiccups,
its lungs practice for its first swallows of air.

Is it true that two might dream the same
dream at the same time?
The fox crosses the meadow, follows its wet nose, trusts
its watery eyes,
passes through us, one inside another inside
another, it slips into the folds of night,
capable of a life without us.

This, an intimacy darker than sex.

3.

I came from the world that was all water, water and darkness
splitting open.

I came from the mallard who dove down into the depths and brought forth
in her beak a clod of silt-mud,
and shook it dry, and began the world
of light and matter.
I spilled from the celestial breast,
the greenish curds out of which crawled worlds and fire and creatures.
I am spun from the wind's loneliness, its longing for bones.
Never again will I be plucked from an oblivious sleeping rib.
Never again will I be carved out of the cartilage
of a man's fear.

4.

Little night tapper, my dreamer and my dream,
my bones will soon turn to water
for you.

My pelvis where your head rocks in its primordial cradle
will ripple and yawn and shock you toward
the white surface.
Small bulge under my right rib, how well
do you know me now?
I only know you in the dark
unlanguaged world.
                              Once in the light,
I know we will never again be this close—
not even skin to skin, lip to nipple,
not when I touch your mysterious sex in the bath,
not when I find my father and your father, both living
in the pools of your eyes.
Not even the words I teach you
will return you
to what you already know, what it means
to come from the watery bone of a dreaming woman.

Somehow, in the passage, the you I speak to
will disappear. Your first name will be lost.
Once born, you will become a vanishing place,
a stranger,

a thing I knew only from inside
a dream.
We will have to begin again.

When I hold you up, slippery and red from the fluid outlet,
fetal yet separate,
and you straighten your legs groundward for the first time;
when I touch the dying cord to cut it,
watching your eyes briefly open, then clamp tight as a boneless thing
in a shell, fearful
for what you have given up;
and provoked to a cry, your grandfather mouth opens,
and in it I glimpse
as it vanishes
our fox blue shadow,
my first words to you from this world
made of milk-curd, pond-mud and bone
will be   *come back*

The Placenta

After he has fallen asleep, after the last nursing
at the end of the undulant dusk when Venus has grown into a solitary
glitter in the western sky and his lips still tug at my nipple,
dreaming it into the smooth cave of his mouth as I carry him
sprawled out and limp from so much milk, as I move and stop
on each step to keep the sleep intact, toward the loft
where the shadows of dusk still shine on the cabin logs;
after I bend to lay him down, careful not to break the deep
and rhythmical breath, careful to transfer the feel of my arms into
the flannel I pack around him, cloth that smells of my milk and
high summer and him; after I watch the eyelids quiver, the lips smack,
the small limbs flinch and stretch as if to awaken but this is
his body settling into the arms of night; then I am free
to go back down and step outside,
and in the first full gasp of nightfall I find I am still thinking
about the placenta,
how strong and sinewy it was, how fast the doctor pulled it out
with rubber gloves and forceps made to fit a baby's head before it was
ready to leave, how he treated it like something worthless
and foul, medical rubbish to be quickly analyzed, disposed of,
when, in fact, I know it should have been paused over, admired, touched
and blessed; I look at the stars forming their nests overhead
and wonder, are you up there somewhere, sure of us
like an angel, like another child I made and lost?

The Sandhill Crane

My feet wet in the dew
I stand at the edge of a draw

in the stillness between dawn
and one June morning. I did not know

what drew me was the sandhill crane
on the other side feeding in tall grass.

She flew across my last dream
in a body not meant to be airborne.

I felt the great spread of her wings
part the air under my eyelids,

her cry, her thin-throated
brain and I awoke

some part of me missing.

Mist rises from the timothy where she
pecks at insects hidden in the long

grass. A moment ago, I almost
made her become something else

but she lifted her tapered wick
of a neck and looked at me

and eye-to-eye there was no mistaking
the delicate head with its splash

of red, the slender beak,
her wrist of a throat

from which a whole world
cries out, wings tucked

until they distrust me enough
to flutter open. She takes me in

then goes back to nibbling
one strand that glistens

and slides between us
in the early light,

the sun up, the moon up,
a bleached bone.

In her mind I'm sure
she was always just herself.

I am the one who
came so close

to changing her
because I do not know myself

not even by my simple cry.

Moonflower

I do not want to be like the moonflower worshipped
for its heavenly scent, its thicksoft white bell
of a petal like a dancing skirt with no
seam, no noticeable zipper. Yes,
I have bowed down

to the moonflower many nights in secrecy, leaving the bedside,
the unlit house, slippering down the late summer street
to a garden where the moonflowers tower
over all else abundant there.
On my knees

before that night altar, I pressed a cheek against the angular unfurl-
ing, the circular opening—its maleness, its femaleness—
and simply gasped in its pure odor.
Like the bees I have
dipped into

the sweet tunnels crazy with a hunger for stickiness, for utter connection.
And I have prayed to its alertness at dawn, the shadows
that form from its name. But to become this, no,
I could not: unreconciled to the sudden
scentless mid-morning wither—

that kind of closure after a night-long bloom.

Birthdream (2)

It is the afterbirth I am after, the afterbirth's
in her not in me.

I must teach her how to get it out,
her first birth, first
loss.

 I must teach her the difference between her
and me and her   but is our breath
separate?

Push with your vaginal muscles. Pull the sad
nest with tenderness with your
two hands. Like this.
Don't mind the glob, the mucous slide, if you get squeamish
you will lose much more than this,
you will not get free of the blur
of me, daughtermother.

This pushing and pulling is good for us. It is not struggle,
but the paradox of our power.

The afterbirth is very old. You cannot force it
to leave. Old and clean,
like a pea-green crone skin washed
out of the sea.

Floating Poem: Manhattan Morning

For the past twenty-four hours rain has filled this city.
Its rivers have stretched their banks like an amphibious thing
growing out of itself, clutching the island, its vertical fogged-in shimmer.
We step into a downpour after a few hours' sleep, the cracks and heaves
in the streets deeply puddled, the sidewalks mostly deserted.
What is an hour in city rain, wet slaps that wipe out the particulars
of street corners, faces, voices, sirens and lights?

We pass the umbrella sellers setting up for another good day,
my arm linked in my mother's, under her strong umbrella,
the one she never needs out west and uses only here
in this city where she's lived her other life.
Umbrellas fill the trash cans along the avenues: the colorful
nylon skins ripped open, some flipped inside-out,
others peeled down to skeletal metal poking the rain,
a hodgepodge of husks and soaked handles.
When she's gone, which part of her will I walk with?
Will I eulogize her shadow? She never prepared me
for continuity, for ordering time into three long blocks.

The city has another odor when it gets wet, everything intense
intensified by rain. Fragrance and stink.
My hands gather smells into my skin: rain and steam
that seeps through a subway grate, the fecal smell
of small autumnal fans dropped by the ginkgo trees, the odor
of the river, fish and waste, the intensity of homeless piss,
recent and stale, morning coffees, round yeasty things
rising in ovens, the beginnings of Chinese soups. Blossom and rot.
How is the rain measured? How do I gauge
the ways we fall not where we need or want to be,
but where we must be? My mother never lived here
yet she is home, leading me from one street to another.
Her eyes shine when she brushes against strangers,
her hair silver with city rain. We walk without direction

yet she knows where she is going. We end up
in front of an apartment building where as a girl
she used to visit her mother. Under the umbrella,
in the morning rain, we stare up at a window
from which for hours she would gaze
across the street to the tower clock on the red brick building
that was a woman's prison, hoping to see a face.
Hoping to shine a light, send something across.

Lupine

Girlhood blue
they still grow tall in the shade
of the aspen
blue link to the summer
of the first kisses
the wind with their prayer, their pollen
in our hard teeth.
They timed their bloom
with the young ruffed grouse learning
to ruffle the air,
solstice coyotes
training their pups to yip.
They still grow bluer than a storm of Junes
bluer than larkspur
earth to all that sky
arid under the sun's first hour
abundant pea family
lips tipped petals we learned
to classify
found other names
bluebonnet quakerbonnet wolfbean
learned to gender wild
flowers they weren't all female
pistil stamen ovary anther
sepal and stem bloomed into
a science   an art   a story
in which we touched
and named a color in us
bold blue bloom
bold blue sweat the sweet
skin of passage
in the back of the field
deep blue
almost violent.

Heartbeat

My pants pushed down around my knees
as the nurse instructed, I regress to schoolgirl twitches.
My still-slim ankles clank the base of the padded
examination table, my fingers twist an unconscious fringe
in the sanitary paper sheet until the doorknob rolls
and the no-eye-contact ob/gyn enters this pink room.
Like a fan across the whole span of my stomach, he opens
his cold manly hand that smells of antiseptic and metal.
Did the boy-skin of his hands understand they could grow
this gnarled and large, did they fathom they would be touching
the bodies of women all day in such sexless ways?
At this stage, my skin cannot fathom stretching past a holiday feast,
rounding to the jump-ball shapes of expectant girls
I saw leave the clinic with cigarettes already in hand.
Where he first spread his palm, the doctor places the ear
of a stethoscope attached to a transistor box. He turns the dial
until the sound of an ocean comes to me, the water of my breath.
And faintly—inside the inside—I have to stop breathing to hear it—
    tictictictictictictictictictictictictictictictictictic...
It's the end of the eighth week, the indifferent period I've read about,
when the labiascrota splits into two words, two worlds,
and I hear it pushing time like a dark clock,
this speck of abstract sex in the fluids,
this sound with its own plan.

Mountain Nocturne

Between the trailer and Purple Mountain
I pass the pelvis of an old death
to scan the grass. Up close,
the white blades bend
with the piss left behind by whatever passed here
in the night, each ruled
by the same sun that orders
my nights into days.

Where did they go, those creatures who made
the sounds that woke me in the night?
The shriek that filled the dark
sleep of the mountain,
the stalked elk-throat, the seemingly gleeful
howls, sharp yips, more of them
and again
the crazed throaty scream
I've held inside since I was a small girl.

How I hated loving them both.
I lay still in a bed shared with an older sister,
my wrists a kindling x across my chest,
listening hard,
torn.
Predator, prey, pray, predator.
I held my breath but my heart kept running.

First Summer

The first time I felt like a mother
it was summer, almost the solstice,
and I had been alone with him
for weeks, lulled into walking
by evening light, still trying
to preserve the dissolving shape
of my former life. Everything I was
was abruptly funneled into infant time:
the unstructured rounds of nursing
and napping, the lamb-like cries
pulling me out of dreamless,
snatched sleeps; the firm gums
wandering from one hill of milk
to the other, small teeth already made
and hidden inside; the eyes still filled
with that other world, unable to find me
across a room; the hand washes
of that tiny miraculous penis;
the sleepers and burper rags; the smell
of his head where light entered
through the sponge of the fontanelle.
Time wove around us an indelible gauze
like mosquito netting, tedious
yet blessed.
                    Storms and clearings.
I bundled him in layers of cloth,
tucked him in the soft pack across my chest,
steadied his head in my palm
like a warmed teacup.
In the dusk, our walking shadow loomed
a long-legged, pregnant shape,
then fell into the hill as we neared the rise.
Catching his scent, the wind sniffed
the new skin and human milk
of him, and came closer.

The sun dropped into the dark ruffle
of mountains as if the earth had swallowed it.
At that moment the wind lunged, a vehement rush,
forced its way down his thin windpipe.
He awoke, jerked back at the neck, swayed
by a gravity greater than the world
of my body. His eyes
widened and bulged, still tearless,
centering me in their fear.
I watched what was invisible
take him with the force
of a swollen current, jaws clenched
and unclenched, I heard the first gasp
of his voice, the cold sleet wind
clutching his delicate throat, an animal
I could not chase away, a spirit
I could not pull back out of him.

Only weeks earlier, in the first tides
of exhaustion, milk, and loss,
I'd flung him sweaty one night
from my arms onto the bed, clasped my hands
behind my neck, gnashed my teeth, and fought off
a fantasy of infanticide, an urge
to take the pillow and squelch
the breath in him, how swift and effortless
I could have done it,
breath my body had labored
to separate from me.
How do I claim that memory, connect
that moment with dusk on the hill-rise
when the wind overcame him
and I rose up with the immense power of a Kali,
of Demeter,
and cupped my hands around his mouth
and turned my back to the wind I love, its darkness,
to make a human windbreak,
to keep a small flame going?

☆
☆ ☆
☆

Birthdream (3)

They lead me by the hand to a room over the barn.
A bed on the planked floor.
A quilt on the bed: sunshine and shadow.
One of them rustles to the dormer, pushes the window
open. A whiff of sagebrush.
One of them pins her net-white prayer cap
to my hair, to help me breathe.
Is she Ella?
Is this how it happened once before, long ago,
on a dark quilt, breathing
prairie?

Floating Poem: Manhattan, Midday

Dressed in patent leather pumps and a wool dress coat
she looked as if she were on her way to lunch,
it being Saturday, midday, the others having taken
their usual table halfway back, out of the window glare
but not too near the swinging door to the kitchen,
already waiting, leaning forward, glancing at wrist watches,
toward the foyer, sipping their Dubonnet and discussing
the fish specials. She was crossing 76th Street
at Columbus, walking south, and here was her coat
spilled under her, turning purple with the winter
grit of the busy street, here were her bone-limp knees.
I pictured the coat and purse her hand still clutched
dispersed on racks at a consignment shop or wherever
clothes and purses end up when someone stops moving
with an abruptness like conception. The pedestrians
formed a circle, clogging the scurry of traffic
until two policemen in bulletproof vests
and the ambulance stormed in and stopped
the siren in the middle of it all.
The paramedics turned her over, pushed
a plastic mask into her face, and we witnessed
how the body when it loses breath is
just that, a body, nothing sacred, nothing more,
not even a trace of fear.
You can't give breath back to someone like that.
So why did we all keep standing there, suspended
from our separate errands to elsewhere, why
did we continue to breathe over her,
glued to the human circle, fixed to the nameless
gray face none of us ever laid eyes on before,
one woman whispering a prayer in Spanish,
another twisting a small gold star between two fingers,
another stroking the ear of a teacup poodle zipped
inside her suede coat, one man shushing another man

who was oblivious and chanting something radiant as he passed;
what made us grow that protective husk
as if to stop the teeming, rude, overwrought
city that suddenly felt like a stranger's thumb squeezing
a wrist to take the pulse?

Birthdream (4)

Clear night and the river sounds closer.
The fir trees rise in a mass over the road,
their spires coming between me and the remote white burrs
of stars.

> I am not used to anything between us. The darkness
> trips me and I lunge downward toward a soft
> wheel rut: the end of winter.

> > In mud my fingers grip the lip of a large boot print.
> > I am a century, feeling my way on knees and hands,

> > > inside something
> > > close to birth.

> > I miss the fierce cold, the squeal of snow
> > my angel shadow....

> In sleep I smell the earth again. If only, in falling,
> we would let ourselves kiss the startled
> skin where we land.

It feels good to be walking alone. To admit to no one
the sound I first heard as the river
is a highway close by, each person encapsulated,
intent on passing swiftly...

Portrait of an Unfinished Self-Portrait

Using the pad of her last clean finger, she smears a storm
of chalk across the eyes. Her bare shoulder
catches the flare of spring from an open door,
a wiggle of lilacs, thighs powdered blue
with dust, the body primary
blue, round as evening on the hill,
an amniotic eighth-month moon.
In her face her mother forms.

She reworks the arc of the back,
the fist bearing down on the bladder.
The viewer can see she would love sex,
fingery smudges, strange tongues,
the *touch me here and here* of the pastel chalks.
           The fetus swirls in the pelvic cap,
               eyes shut, not complete,
            crowded by mermaid sisters
             who brush each other's hair
                brush out a father's
                  tangled kisses.
When she moves you feel all of them,
mysterious little bumps that surface
and sink away.

Think

I will never understand what made our father think
of it, what made him think it would work,
this punishment he pushed so deep into my brother,
over and over—his schoolboy wrist, his fingers smaller
than the fat red pencil he had to push
across the tablet writing the word Think
one-hundred Think two-hundred Think
three-hundred times each time he failed
to think to please our father. The aftersilence
lingered in the house like old smoke. After the scolding,
the whipping, the pencil clutched in the boy's hand
to remedy stupidity, my brother had to print that word
perfectly, I think he failed at this too, he had to think
each time he wrote it not to smudge the word
on the line above, not to press too hard, snap the lead.
He had to think so many times in vertical columns it made
a permanent vertigo in him, and ever since
he has been trying to drive home in a whiteout.

I wanted to take each Think, dunk them in sludge
and brush them across my father's teeth to make him think
and remember how it felt the time his mother soaped his mouth
for saying "it's hot as hell in here" one summer day when it was
hot as hell and they were too poor to buy a fan.
Did he think his punishment more intelligent than soaping
out a simile? I think of the words that might have freed my brother:

Tink as in the meticulous crawl of lead.
Hide as in the accomplice.
Ink as in the soul's liquid.
Name as in the forgotten lesson.
Kin as in you can never escape from him.

What does it mean when the names for our feelings stop
bubbling onto our tongues? The meaning
of the word breaks down over time like a carcass in prairie grass,
it decays under the monotony to pure sound, and then to less
than sound, and then to shapes:
damaged liver, smudge in a dreamscape, escape
in a spill of ink, bottle,
numb migraine.

Morning in the Boiling River

1.

At daybreak we strip and enter it,
let ourselves bubble and spin, drift
into silence in the roar
of two rivers.

One river is continual snowmelt,
a trickle east and west down the divide,
a rush across caldera grass.
It stings and if you sit in it long
past numbness,
you could live to be a hundred, or die
by noon of hypothermia.

The other river, white as ash and boiling,
comes straight from the gut, rages
out of a yellowish gash
in the earth and smells
like an ancient egg. Full-strength this river
burns human skin
yet patches of arnica and purple death camus
bloom in its swifts.

As we soak in the fast blur of the two,
the split self coalesces,
a braid of fire and ice. Healing
is a coming together
of opposites.

2.

How I love it when the mind finally shrinks
to its first size, smaller than
a man's scrotum soaking in the pure

cold current. When thinking curls up
like the beautiful shrivel
of the lopped-off umbilical cord,
no longer necessary
for living.

That's when the senses spill the soul.

The body becomes this confluence,
the head a crown of morning—
sounds, smells, tastes,
touches and vision.

I no longer close my eyes
to see what I need
to see.

The gnarls of a tumor dissolve, float away,
the hair grows back
white and thick in the ears.

This river spins a lost man,
makes him fertile again, runs
the history of liquor
from his skin.

This river midwifes us, slick arch of the back,
blood, wrinkles of fingers,
new skin
among the blooms of camus and arnica.

And all morning, as it happens,
the elk drift across,
oblivious,
dropping their necks to take long drinks.

The Amish Midwife

When she comes home to the farm after a birth,
her children grown and scattered into their own homes
down the road, her husband dead since last November, she sits
and breathes into the emptiness of the house as if to fill it.
At first the breath is visible, the room cold
from her eighteen-hour night—
the grunts and wails of the woman, the work to make her walk
and stay upright, the asking of things from the husband to keep him
busy: clean cloths, sterilized scissors, hot water, hot tea,
another pillow, quiet the dogs, comfort the children
who have never heard their mother in labor.
Just as it takes a newborn some time to fully enter the world,
it has taken her man a long time to fully leave. She can feel him slipping
as the seasons outgrow themselves, the unplowed fields
turning spongy, the worms surfacing in furrows.
She breathes the wood smell, the soap, the earthy smell of placenta
and umbilicus not quite scrubbed off her hands. But breath
won't fill an emptiness such as here in this house.
It only marks it like starlight on a cold shed
until his absence becomes the thing she returns to,
and she has almost grown used to it, even those things
she hasn't touched—his hats on the hall tree,
the toy tractor collection on the high shelf in the sitting room,
the tools worn smooth by his hands
in the clapboard shed where she, back from a difficult birth,
found him with a strong white rope around his neck.

New Moon, End of October

Morning met the grass in whiteness
white sparks, chalk and
bone.

noon was a gristle of crickets.

dusk was black leaf smoke, quick, then dark,
star-still, darker
still.

November

How long did I overlook November?
All her seeds and smoke,
the unloved silk of weeds,
her puzzle strewn across the path,
her reticence, all her children,
all her withering skins.

Time to say goodbye to the marsh and forest,
all stumps and stagnant water and final stillness.
Time to thank the lost hands
that held the shade above me,
made me soft and hidden,
part of the grass, a calm smudge
in the twists of summer.
Time to miss the leaves,
the crude bench made by a lover's hands,
the frogs that thrumped
the sound I carry primal in my ears,
the dull marsh stones drifting
under thin dreams of ice.

I never heard the iron sound
of centuries lugged away,
but I touch what's left, flat stumps,
sliced nuclei, beautiful broken
rings, origins
of something gone, that first moment
when seeds gather spines
and density from the soil.

Farther, I find work of a beaver,
a terraced spire, inner wood where
the muscular teeth halved a complete birch,

took what was needed
and left the gnawed trunk to rot.
I run my fingers across the rippled memory
of its mouth,
I carry the dark intelligence of its paws,
I touch the evidence
as wind touches winter in the land,
longing for wholeness, for the dead to assure us
they're not lonely.

How long will the yellow apple hang,
the last worm-burrowed heart
of the orchard, how long
the thin, gnarled leaf
like the chafed elbow of an old woman,
how much longer?

And the deer
strapped to anything that carries them,
the buck with mouth open,
blood drips from the tongue,
the doe with her small limp neck bloodied
with the tongue-blood of the buck,
the bodies twined like doomed
lovers, the eyes unshuttable,
spiritless and dark and looking back.

These dusks come swift and early,
the stars brighten and multiply,
the nights thick with their cold perfume.
The moon reaches down to roots
and in the trees all the nests
begin to show. Here are openings,
disclosures, as when a woman comes
to see too deeply into her life
and chooses to go the other way.
She lets the frost gather on her feet,

the wind scatter her thin seeds,
and takes only what she needs:
the deep red berries in her skirts,
the cold retina of silence,
everything dead and forgivable.

Birthdream (5)

Just before dawn my father came to say goodbye.
It was not a spoken goodbye, it was not
the brush of a whisker across a sleeping cheek. No,
it was the silent pull of eyes,
it was a small nest with strands of human
and horse hair, grass from the upper meadow,
placed near my head and filled
with the eggs of a music that won't translate
into daylight. The embered liver
of the night scattered into the cold
mud of the river. Music thrashed in me
until I had to awaken to release it. I awoke
to the sound of someone sleeping,
the black cricket in the grass beneath the sill,
the summer gone. My father was still alive.
He was arranging the last act,
the one in which a woman breaks
a golden song from stone.

Venus

I stand waist-deep in the grass, holding my infant son in my arms,
waiting for her. His small arm squirms,
pushing away from me like an oar stirring the lazy currents
of the evening air, the other slumps between
my elbow and swollen breast.
The dusk of midsummer has spun us into its gloss,
our shadow huge across the hill
and on the mountains glimmer the old high snows.
His arms flail once as if the spirit part of him, wild ghost
that enters slowly through the pulse of the fontanelle,
were still getting used to its small bones.
I rest my palm on his scalp to feel this spirit;
it did not come from me.

Then his arms, legs and neck drop limp,
satiated, plump from nine months of my blood,
two months of my milk, dusk, the last drops
shining on his cheeks as sleep creeps into every cell
of his body like nightfall crawling across the wide sky.
His fists unfurl like the smooth white skirts of the moonflowers
that open summer nights around the obelisk,
beginning to trust this world. I trace his palms,
roads drawn from a long winter inside me.

I glance from him to that place in the sky
where nightly she appears, stark goddess and planet,
the one who both binds and unbinds us, and back to him.
Who is he, this stranger pulled from me?
Whose tiny mouth, the hump of the milk blister
at the tip of his upper lip,
lips I've seen search for a nipple along the arm of anyone
who holds him; and whose is this automatic tongue
rooting in its sleep, mistaking the night wind
for the known beat of my breast?

Does the sadness in his larynx come from me?
From whom did he take the smell and fuzz of his head,
the intricate veins in his ears? The wombed haze
of his eyes that cannot yet find himself in a mirror,
the navel that tightened and closed around the last scrap
of umbilicus until the blood cord of me-to-him
was lost—from whom do these come? And whose penis,
that most foreign part I pulled from my unconscious,
unreconciled, blue behind the umbilicus; penis I avoided
those first weeks, shy of it, hesitant to touch,
smaller than the tip of my smallest finger,
stretched and sculpted from clitoral cells
the eighth week in utero. And from whom
comes the thick perfect seam of the scrotum, vulva
sewn into one lovely sac, dangling like the soft
unused flesh under an old woman's arm?

At last he is sleeping the only sleep that untethers me
from him, the Venus sleep.
The night grass hushes the last of the day,
the shadows across the hills darken into one inseparable wash
and I watch her coming toward us, boldest of lights
in the western sky. She comes close, closer,
to teach me how to love, and I hold him up,
this sleeping child whose milk-fat cheek
I turn toward her
as an offering, as something to shine
and give back.

Jenny Marie

This morning I am thinking of Jenny Marie, of being nine
and already having to live with the beginnings
of breasts, of being too young
and self-conscious

for a first bra yet too tender there near the hinge
of the sternum to ignore their wild coming.
I am thinking of how I looked
then looked away

not wanting to add to her already bloodstrong awareness, and of
linkage: the small brown potatoes her grandfather,
father, brothers, and uncles cultivate in this
dry soil, the chemical

plumage of the yellow crop duster I heard just after sunrise,
how it woke me nosing toward the ground as if it
longed to plunge into the undulant
green shimmer,

and how her mother who's had two mastectomies this past
winter, six months apart with intensive chemo
in between, has this morning a will
of beauty

about her face, a cared-for radiance like the yellow-breasted
meadowlark perched on the broken wing
of the windmill to sing something
remarkable—it is

tempting to call it a song, an intricate trill I cannot
make as suddenly it decides to lift its brilliant
larkish body skyward
and off.

Summerless

The lake is so cold the man from Bavaria
is the only one who swims in it and only
because he is practicing for the northern
bay water of the Pacific. Late,
in the field, a handful of lightning bugs.
Too chilled to flit about, they huddle
in the grass, morse-coding a calculated
message to the kidnapped summer.
What could their fires change, brief
as a girl's love for a gaudy ring found
by its shine in the bottom silt? Snuffed
green lanterns, powerless
heat asleep in the wings.
Yet they are what haunts me
as the summer passes.

Floating Poem: Manhattan Night
When I Loved Mr. Hoberman

I said it to the night, to the building across the street,
the two lit globes atop the pillars, the crouching gnomes
that hold the worlds up, marbled beehives and stars.
I said it to the ginkgo tree beyond the balcony,
the homeless person whose face I couldn't see sleeping
under a slip of plastic in the corridor.
I said it not to him but to his shoes, to the human shape
in the woodgrain on the door.
My throat would break, my breasts collapse,
my tongue sink if I didn't.
I said it to the quiet hour, so brief in such a city,
to the starlight I could not see, to the moon that already knew,
the ceiling fan and the summer night as it brushed my knees,
I said it to the Avenue, the drooping iris, the out-of-season oranges
on the sidewalk of the Korean deli,
to the caged bird, the cello, the grand piano
in the one-room apartment below. I said it to the pillow,
to the smell of me on my fingers
in the middle of the night
in the middle of the night
when no one heard.

☆
☆
☆

Milk

Given your birth, I am the glue of the cosmos. Love, I am
what wakes you, puts you to sleep, keeps you going.
I am fluid matter, essential as swallows
of air.

Out of love for you I spew a breezy spray from a zillion flesh-cracks.
I made the thick white path across the night.
I made the pillow smell of you.
I made your muscles and dreams thicken with meaning.

Do you know I created a world out of a chapped nipple?
Do you know I made the hills round (you thought it was wind and erosion).
I even made the neck bone
of the moon.

So charged is my love, when I hear you cry I surge toward you
like an electrical current. When you are brought near me
I tingle and pulse. Even the curdled smell of me
in your sleepy mouth makes me rise up. Tongue to teat,
this is my love for you.

I am ordained as the stickiness between you and your mother
That cellular blur, that cave of sleeping eggs, sperm sacs, the elixir
when you focus and find the eyes,
the sudden union.

When you sniff me out with eyes shut, wiggle fingers and toes,
wag your head, latch on like a pup and suck, I come
oozing out of both breasts, out of all the udders, teats,
cracks, and you slurp and squeal like a pig in paradise:
this is my pleasure and purpose.

I will dry up and seem not to matter only when you turn away
with the teeth I made for you, with your hunger
for other things. You may think I am full
of myself, but you are wrong.
It is you who is full of me. I am nothing
without you. I am your marrow.

Never forget me.

Union

When she combs her hair morning and evening
evening and morning she does not remember when she
combs her hair with her eyes shut
her small chin forced up with each pull of the brush
her neck veins taut she does not remember when she drinks
the water just after midnight
and at noon her thirst returning she does not
remember she does not remember

their faces framed on the dresser
in the mirror side by side
his plum hand on the Lego boat
his apricot hand around the bottle she does not
remember   their eyes are not shut
they are not asleep   they are not awake
they are   *we are*

weeping
        she does not remember a before   only an after
we've all wept   *into water*

she could have set the house on fire in our sleep
        lit one match
                burned herself
                      and run
she could have made a mother of fire

the water's gasp
        she does not remember hearing
only the sound of birds in her head
a small flock in the leaf-bare tree
singing in unison *we are here we are here*
lost voices *we are free*
        bless us
          forgive us

we've all lived in an oval of water
we've all been a bloody head

other nights she drove to the water's edge
switched off the headlights
        listened to their breathing
                wept and lit a cigarette
our eyes are not shut
        we are not asleep
                we are not awake

              listened to the pond frogs
burping for love she
        does not remember
            the water's gasp

water to air
    the part of her that first effaced
        expelled them

the tilt of the neck
        made breath
            air to water
sending them back
      water to water
        sending us back

she does not remember
        the shine of hair the car
            the water's gasp

the cruel air she breathed
      effortlessly
          all along
            the dark walk back

☆
☆   ☆

Nightfall

In the tall summer grass
I hear the teeth of field mice
still at work.
All birds jostle for the sound podium.
The clumsy grouse glubs along the sage, claiming
the first strata of sky.
The sandhill crane and the great
moon-faced owl
claim whole shadows,
streambeds and ravines.

Close by, I watch a small brown bird,
fledgling of the mountain blue bird,
settle on the eye socket
of a horse skull I once pulled from dried mud.
I recognize it as the same bird
my year-old son found this morning,
limp on the deck beneath the window,
only moments before the dogs got to it.
How proudly he toddled toward me,
hands shining
under the dead wings.

Now the young bird,
defiant of death, has come back
to dance along the bleached white skull.
It has come back to bestow a blessing
on the child
who is falling asleep upstairs,
wings fluttering under the thin
dress of eyelids.

☆
☆
☆

lullaby

whose
wisp of moon
whose smile whispers
in the fat mimosa branch
whose white wheel blooms over green hill
whose hush in the folding wings
whose hooting owls
whose hush
whose fire of moonflowers
whose harvest of stars
whose cold garden
september sky
october sky
november sky
whose cheek sleeps
on the shoulder
of winter
whose

From A Little Handbook on Dreams

If there are dreams I should remember
            they have long since gone
                        where dreams go

                        when the eyes blink them under

It was somewhere near here
            this certain
            dream

                        not an animal but the feeling
                                    of one who has come
                                                to the edge of the dark trees

                        stops
                                    lifts its quiet neck
                                    and knows

                        I am on the path
            an animal only another can smell

What woke me
            which part of the anatomy
                        of the dream?

            I take the silence
                        into my mouth: it is small
                                    smooth and dry

                        a pebble I suck
                        to find water

someone fills a white bowl
        places it on the sill
                trough on the dream path

Sleeping, I feel the heat of his body
        as if there were a sun
        in him

        the heat of his body
                asleep
                        as if he were pregnant

                we dream
                        hand in hand
                        more than a human shadow.

Nightfall

I blink, and the sun has swept up the last shadows
and gone inside.
In a vast dark circle
seven hundred mountains are coming to life.
They fuse and grow, stretch and float
the silence toward me.
I think of a small act,
the rodent jaw bones, teeth intact,
I plucked earlier from the grass.

I rub my fingers across them,
place the upper and lower together
to form one side of a mouth,
sky to purple granite,
a small wholeness
out of half of it.

The night grass shivers in my knees,
the silence taking all of me
into its mouth.

Acknowledgments

Grateful acknowledgment is made to the editors of the publications in which the following poems first appeared.

Blue Mesa Review: "The Placenta" and "Afternoon Along the Firehole River";

The Kenyon Review: "Think" and "September First";

The New Yorker: "Birthdream (1)";

Nimrod International Journal: "The Amish Midwife";

Ploughshares: "New Moon, End of October";

Poetry: "Summerless";

The Southern Review: "Prelude" and "Floating Poem: Manhattan Morning";

West Branch: "Birthdream (5)," "November" and "The Sandhill Crane";

Yellow Silk: "Jenny Marie" and "Milk."

Lines from the poem, "Yes, But," by James Wright, from *This Journey*, © 1982 by Anne Wright, executrix of the Estate of James Wright. Reprinted with the permission of Random House.

I am grateful to the MacDowell Colony, the Virginia Center for the Creative Arts, and the Ucross Foundation for their facilities and support; my time at each of these places was significant in the development of this book. I also wish to thank the Artist-in-Residence Program at Yellowstone National Park, the Pennsylvania Council on the Arts, the Virginia Commission on the Arts, and James Madison University for assistance which allowed me to complete this book. Grateful acknowledgment is also made to A. Poulin, Jr., for his warm response to these poems in the last months of his life.

The poem, "Portrait of an Unfinished Self-Portrait," owes its origins to the painting, "Seventh Month," by Miriam Garcia. The title and poem, "From *A Little Handbook on Dreams*," was influenced in part by *A Little Book on the Human Shadow* by Robert Bly, edited by William Booth, and *A Little Course in*

Dreams by Michael Kohn. I am indebted to *Of Woman Born*, by Adrienne Rich, and to *Memories, Dreams, and Reflections* by Carl Jung; these books became my teachers.

My sincere thanks to Kevin Reynolds for his reciprocity in childcare, and to Susan Facknitz, Miriam Garcia, and Mindy Weinreb for their critical and sensitive readings of this book in its first form. And, perpetually, my gratitude to Rita Gabis, wise friend and this book's midwife.

About the Author

Laurie Kutchins is the author of a previous collection of poems, *Between Towns*, winner of the Texas Tech University Press's First Book Poetry Competition for 1991. She is Visiting Assistant Professor of English at the University of New Mexico at Albuquerque.

BOA EDITIONS, LTD.

AMERICAN POETS CONTINUUM SERIES

Vol. 1   *The Fuhrer Bunker: A Cycle of Poems in Progress*
W. D. Snodgrass

Vol. 2   *She*
M. L. Rosenthal

Vol. 3   *Living With Distance*
Ralph J. Mills, Jr.

Vol. 4   *Not Just Any Death*
Michael Waters

Vol. 5   *That Was Then: New and Selected Poems*
Isabella Gardner

Vol. 6   *Things That Happen Where There Aren't Any People*
William Stafford

Vol. 7   *The Bridge of Change: Poems 1974–1980*
John Logan

Vol. 8   *Signatures*
Joseph Stroud

Vol. 9   *People Live Here: Selected Poems 1949–1983*
Louis Simpson

Vol. 10   *Yin*
Carolyn Kizer

Vol. 11   *Duhamel: Ideas of Order in Little Canada*
Bill Tremblay

Vol. 12   *Seeing It Was So*
Anthony Piccione

Vol. 13   *Hyam Plutzik: The Collected Poems*

Vol. 14   *Good Woman: Poems and a Memoir 1969–1980*
Lucille Clifton

Vol. 15   *Next: New Poems*
Lucille Clifton

Vol. 16   *Roxa: Voices of the Culver Family*
William B. Patrick

Vol. 17   *John Logan: The Collected Poems*

Vol. 18   *Isabella Gardner: The Collected Poems*

Vol. 19   *The Sunken Lightship*
Peter Makuck

Vol. 20   *The City in Which I Love You*
Li-Young Lee

Vol. 21   *Quilting: Poems 1987–1990*
Lucille Clifton

Vol. 22   *John Logan: The Collected Fiction*

Vol. 23   *Shenandoah and Other Verse Plays*
Delmore Schwartz

Vol. 24   *Nobody Lives on Arthur Godfrey Boulevard*
Gerald Costanzo

Vol. 25   *The Book of Names: New and Selected Poems*
Barton Sutter

Vol. 26   *Each in His Season*
W. D. Snodgrass

Vol. 27   *Wordworks: Poems Selected and New*
Richard Kostelanetz

Vol. 28   *What We Carry*
Dorianne Laux

Vol. 29   *Red Suitcase*
Naomi Shihab Nye

Vol. 30   *Song*
Brigit Pegeen Kelly

Vol. 31   *The Fuehrer Bunker: The Complete Cycle*
W. D. Snodgrass

Vol. 32   *For the Kingdom*
Anthony Piccione

Vol. 33   *The Quicken Tree*
Bill Knott

Vol. 34   *These Upraised Hands*
William B. Patrick

Vol. 35   *Crazy Horse in Stillness*
William Heyen

COLOPHON

The Night Path, poems by Laurie Kutchins, has been set using digitized Monotype Dante fonts and published in a first edition of 500 copies in hardcover and 2,000 in paperback.

The Isabella Gardner Poetry Award is given biennially to a poet in mid-career whose manuscript is of exceptional merit. Poet, actress, and associate editor of *Poetry* magazine, Isabella Gardner (1915–1981) published five celebrated collections of poetry, was three times nominated for the National Book Award, and was the first recipient of the New York State Walt Whitman Citation of Merit for Poetry. She championed the work of young and gifted poets, helping many of them find publication.